Festivals

GRAHAM OWEN and ALISON SEAMAN

WAYLAND

Festivals
Jesus and Mary
Special Occasions
Worship

Editors: Carron Brown
Series consultant: Alison Seaman
Designer and typesetter: Jean Wheeler
Cover designer: Steve Wheele Design
Picture researcher: Gina Brown

First published in 1998 by Wayland Publishers Ltd,
61 Western Road, Hove, East Sussex, BN3 1JD

British Library Cataloguing in Publication Data
  Seaman, Alison
  Worship. - (Looking at Christianity)
  1. Fasts and feasts - Juvenile literature
  I.Title II. Owen, Graham
  263.9

ISBN 0 7502 2238 7

Picture acknowledgements
Andes Press Agency/Robert J. Bennett 8, /Carlos Reyes-Manzo 5, 7, 9, 10, 14, 16 (bottom), 26; The Bridgeman Art Library, London/ Museo de San Marco dell'Angelico, Florence, Italy 17; J. Allan Cash 20; John Crook/*Pentecost*, Batik banner by Thetis Blacker, Winchester Cathedral 23; Dorling Kindersley 16 (top); Eye Ubiquitous/Bennett Dean 6; Getty Images/Oliver Benn 27, /Terry Vine 15, /Craig Wells 1; Sonia Halliday 18, Robert Harding 22, /ASAP & S. Avrilsar 19, /Jeremy Bright 24; Panos Pictures/Paul Smith 13; Wayland Picture Library 4, /Penny Davies 6, 21, /Chris Fairclough 11, /Zak Waters 12, /Tim Woodcock 25.

Cover photo by Martyn F. Chillmaid

Printed and bound by EuroGrafica S.p.A., Italy

Contents

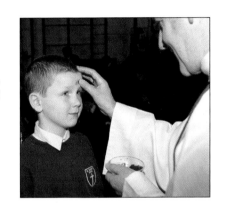

All religious words are explained in the glossary.

Festivals are special times when we like to get together with our friends.

On these festival days Christians remember Jesus and his followers. They celebrate their faith on these special days.

4

Festivals help Christians remember important events in Jesus's life.

Jesus lived a long time ago. Christians believe that Jesus is the Son of God. Every year, all around the world, Christians prepare for festivals together.

Michael is opening the first door on his Advent calendar.

The calendar helps him to count the days to Christmas. Advent is the time when Christians look forward to the festival of Christmas.

Josh is lighting a candle on the Advent ring.

There are four coloured candles, one for each Sunday of Advent. Josh and Emma will light the white candle in the middle of the ring on Christmas Day.

Christmas

It is Christmas Day. Robert, Lisa and John are opening their presents.

Christmas is a time for giving presents. They can't wait to give their mum and dad the special gifts they have made for them. And, of course, they want to open their presents.

Katie and Ruth are making a picture about the birth of Jesus.

They read in the Bible that Jesus was born in a stable in Bethlehem. Christians believe that Jesus is God's gift to all the world.

Mark, Jason and Tom are acting in their school Christmas play.

They are shepherds. In the Bible, three shepherds were told by an angel to go to Bethlehem to look for a newborn baby who was the son of God. They must have been very excited to hear this good news.

Ben and Paul are kings in their play.

They are wearing splendid costumes. The kings brought gifts to Jesus in the stable. Paul is the king who brings Jesus a gift of gold. It is a special gift for a special baby.

Toby is tossing a pancake for his pancake party.

It is Shrove Tuesday, a day for having a good time. Tomorrow Lent begins and Toby and his family will start thinking about Easter, the most important Christian festival.

The season of Lent lasts forty days. It is a time to prepare for Easter.

Lent is a quiet time after the fun of Shrove Tuesday. Christians spend time thinking about how God wants them to live their lives.

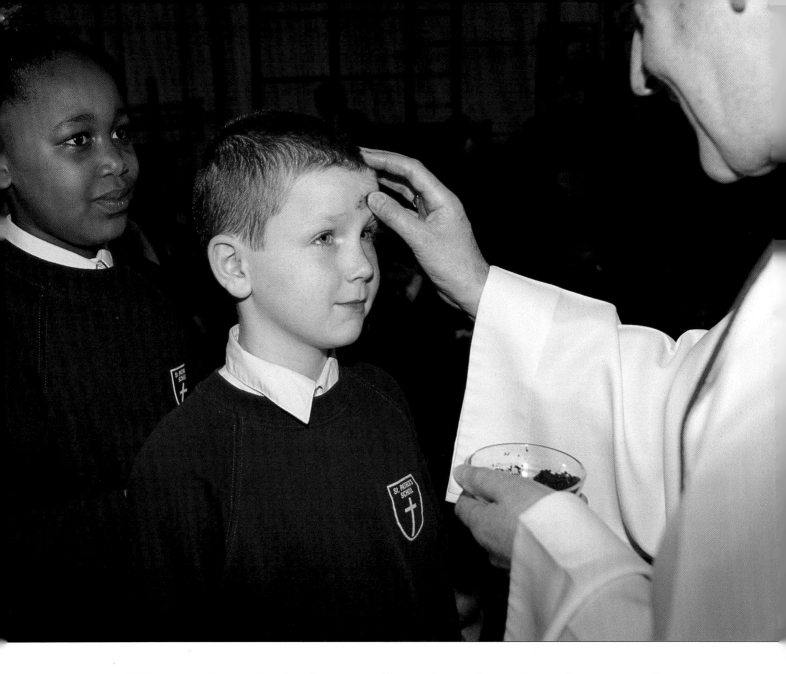

The priest is using ash to make the shape of the cross on Simon's forehead.

This ceremony takes place on Ash Wednesday, the first day of Lent. It reminds Christians that God still loves them and forgives them even when things go wrong.

Lisa has given her mum a bunch of flowers for Mothering Sunday.

During Lent there is a special day for mothers. Lisa has helped to make posies of flowers to be given out in church on Mothering Sunday.

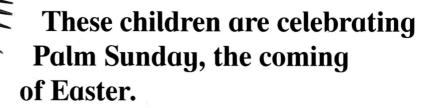

These children are celebrating Palm Sunday, the coming of Easter.

On Palm Sunday, Christians remember the time when Jesus rode into Jerusalem on a donkey. Everyone was pleased to see him, and waved palm branches to welcome him.

Christians remember the last meal Jesus had with his friends.

Jesus told them that he wouldn't be with them for long. When they shared the meal of bread and wine, he told them to remember him whenever they did this together.

Good Friday is the saddest day of the Christian year.

Christians remember that some people turned against Jesus and wanted to kill him. He was put to death on a cross.

These people are helping to carry a cross around their town in Israel.

This is a way for people to remember that Jesus died on a cross. Christians believe he was willing to die for them.

# Easter Day

Easter is here. A new day begins.

Christians believe that Jesus came back to life.
As they watch the sun rise on Easter Day, they
remember that Jesus brings them new life.

Pentecost

After Jesus had gone to heaven, his friends did not know what to do.

At Pentecost, Christians remember that God helped Jesus's friends by giving them the gift of the Holy Spirit. This made them brave again and they wanted to go and tell everyone about Jesus.

Harvest festival

Christians believe that God made the world.

Christians know that God loves and cares for the world. He expects everyone to help look after his wonderful creation.

Michael and Kim have brought Harvest gifts to their church.

Christians give thanks for all of God's gifts on this special day. They bring gifts to say thank you to God for all the good things in life.

Saints' days

Christians remember special people, like Mary the mother of Jesus.

On Saints' Days, Christians say thank you to God for their lives. Some saints are well known, some are not. Since the time of Jesus, all Christians have tried to be like him.

Every Sunday is a festival day.

Even though Jesus is no longer alive, Christians believe he is with them when they share bread and wine together.

Index